Business Advertising – Afrikaans Edition

By Arthur H Tafero

Includes lesson plans

Forward

I am a professor of marketing because I enjoy it immensely. I love watching the creativity of my university students develop from observers to proactive marketing maniacs. Some get it and others do not; just like in real life on Madison Avenue. I had the good fortune to fail at advertising at a very tender age (18) and retreat into cost accounting on Wall Street. I was more comfortable with numbers. I just did not have the creativity it took to go to the next level of my advertising agency. We parted on friendly terms and I learned a lot while I was there.

In 1965, advertising was still a business in its developmental stages. TV advertising was still a mystery to most advertising agencies on Madison Avenue at the time. Olgilvy and Mather seemed to be quite good at it, but many other agencies floundered in that venue. There were no computers to do easy research then. Everything had to be done with books, libraries and going out to take surveys. Research was a bit more physically demanding then. There were no cell phones to store data. You did a lot of writing on yellow note pads. Researchers used to get cramps in their hands from taking so many notes.

There was no internet, no Wikipedia, no search engines or even a place to store data. Data processing was kept on keypunch cards and printed out on bulky paper that went on and on with boring black on white numbers and text. You could go blind or go to sleep just reading them for one hour. Every company had files; and I mean a LOT of files. Paper files. A place like Metropolitan Life Insurance had FLOORS of offices that had nothing but paper files. How people could work there and maintain their sanity was beyond me.

Yep, advertising was still an inexact science (and still is for that matter) in 1965. There were clumsy TV ads with dancing cigarette boxes of Chesterfield, terrible radio spots with some academic (like myself) coming on to EXPLAIN why you should buy a certain product that would increase your brain capacity, lackluster newspaper ads that had no captions under their pictures or headlines for their ad, and some really horrendous billboards on the way down to Florida that practically had half the Constitution written on them while you were driving past at sixty miles an hour and had about five seconds to read it.

Advertising has come a long way since then, but it is important not to forget the basics of great advertising, which I believe David Ogilvy had captured in his classic text, *Confessions of an Advertising Man,* one of the books I use to teach my university students at YUFE (Yunnan University of Finance and Economics), one of the leading Chinese universities for business in the entire country. And if you haven't noticed lately, China and its economic savvy have obliterated all other countries in GDP in the last ten years. To be sure, there are still weaknesses in the Chinese economy (as there are in all economies), but Chinese students are born with the entrepreneur gene (over 5% of the population has tried to start a new business); that is over 65 million businesses.

The downside of that number is that 92% of these businesses fail within three years according to the business loan departments at the Bank of China. However, that does not stop the next wave of soldiers from going over the top directly into the machine gun fire of the business world. As in war, no one ever thinks that they will be the next one to fall in the line of fire.

Three primary reasons for the failure of over 90% of all small businesses in China are the following; (1) poor advertising, (2) poor technology skills, as in creating and maintaining a web site that develops a dependable revenue stream, and (3) a distinct lack of understanding of the importance of having a niche, or very unique approach. These and many other issues and principles of good advertising will be discussed in the following lesson plan outlines. Hope you profit from the content.

Arthur H Tafero
Writer
Amazon.com
Professor of Marketing
Yunnan University School of Finance and Economics
Owner
AskMrMovies.com

Table of Contents

Business Advertising

Course Outline

This course outline for Business Advertising will include, but not be limited to, the following: Clarity of Objective, Desired Roles of Advertising, Target Segmentation, Clarity of Message, Reasons to Buy, Credibility of Value Proposition, Desired Consumer Action, Relativity of Target's Mindset, Choice of Medium, PPC (pay per click), SEO (search engine optimization) word selection, advertising design, advertising elements, and an examination of classic advertising suggestions from a master of the art, David Ogilvy. Included areas are: How to Manage an Advertising Agency, How to Get Clients, How to Keep Clients, How to Build Great Campaigns, How to Write Potent Copy and others. Also included in the course will be four lessons concentrating on the issues of advertising and sales in China.

Primary Teaching Text:

Confessions of an Advertising Man – David Ogilvy

Instructor: Arthur H Tafero, MA, Columbia University

Intro to Lesson One

So you want to be in advertising. You saw every episode of *Mad Men* and it made you yearn for the chance to be the next Donald Draper. Forget it; it's just a TV show and it is at least fifty years behind the times. It was before cell phones, computers, the internet, DVDs, Cable TV, CDs, and a host of other technological advances that make almost everything on the show obsolete. Companies had no web sites. Revenue streams and SEO problems were inconceivable.

However, when it came to capturing the human element of advertising, *Mad Men* pretty much is in a league of its own and extremely accurate. Advertising execs are ruthless, greedy, ambitious to a fault, obsessed, driven and more. Some have ethics, but most do not. You will have to decide for yourself how ethical you will be. Can be ethical and still make scads of money? David Ogilvy did and that is why I am using him as a role model. His book clearly illustrates that the advertising business is not all fun and games. Why do people do it? Because if you are successful, you will make ten times the money someone working in an office or a educational institution makes.

Here is a lesson plan outline that examines some basic principles of advertising.

Lesson 1 – General Advertising Elements

1 . Clarity of Objective: What is the reason why you are advertising, what is it that you are out to achieve – this should be very clear because this is the foundation for the creation of the advertising campaign. SRS Value Bazaar may like to position itself as the place for the finest products and prices. Whereas, Exxon may like to reassure people on the eco-friendly approach of their business.

2. Desired Role of Advertising: Do you want to introduce a new product or service? Do you want to drive up the imagery of your brand? Do you want the brand to take a leadership role? Do you want your brand to engage its consumers? Do you wish to drive up trials? Do you wish to change perceptions? Put your finger on this first so that you can push the right lever.

3. Target Segmentation: Who are the people you wish to speak in a focused manner – it pays to build in their needs and aspirations, motivators, attitude, outlook into your communication. Am I looking at youngsters who are looking for a new hip pub, or am I talking a young family man who is a prime target for my Insurance product?

4. Clarity of Message: clarity also includes crisp single-mindedness of your proposition. Remember it is the single-mindedness of the proposition, whose building components may be more than one. The bigger picture in messaging should not be five different things, but instead about the potent thing that is the result of those five different things.

5. Reason to buy: the reason why you think your target set will find your brand offering different, relevant, exciting, problem-solving, inviting...

6. Credibility of value-proposition. Crucial, if you don't want people to flip the page or zap the channel.

7. Desired consumer action: What is it that you wish him to do as a result of your communication: feel confident after using your product, think better of you, visit your store, buy online, ask for a demo...

8. Relativity with the target set's current mindset. If in today's scenario people want capital preservation first, then this would not be the time to peddle a high-risk, high-return small-cap mutual fund.

9. Choice of Medium: TV, web, newspapers & magazines, radio... Their attributes and consumption behavior by consumers define the kind of advertising, sometimes impact it at the very conceptual stage. The bandwidth offered by the combination audio, video, web and graphics can be spectacular.

10. Space and need for vivid exaggeration, metaphors, unexpected treatment, starkness. Nothing plain stands out too much, you need to build in some highpoints.

11. Bids for PPC (pay per click) campaigns

12. Budgets PPC compaigns

Without these two elements concept of success and greater ROI can never be achieved. How do you find the best bid and budget for your PPC campaign?

Some PPC management services that will help you out in managing your campaigns

• Managing costs
• Investigating into the value of a click
• Knowing when to stop spending more
• Running budgets well
• Operating the bidding system strategically

However, while starting your campaigns two questions must be entertained properly are

       a.   How can we generate high-quality leads ?

       b.   How can we generate high volumes of leads?

Maintaining balance between these two questions will become the key for bid and budget for any of your PPC campaigns.

ICA and HW 1

Answer the following essays

    1.   How can you generate high-quality leads?
    2.   How should we choose our medium for advertising?
    3.   Why is target segmentation important in advertising?
    4.   What is the desired role of advertising?

Additional Internet Resources for this Lesson:

General Resource

http://www.askmrmovies.com

Crazy People (1990) Great Dudley Moore movie about advertising

Professional Advertising

shinyads.com/solutions/self-serve-pro/

Elements of Adverting

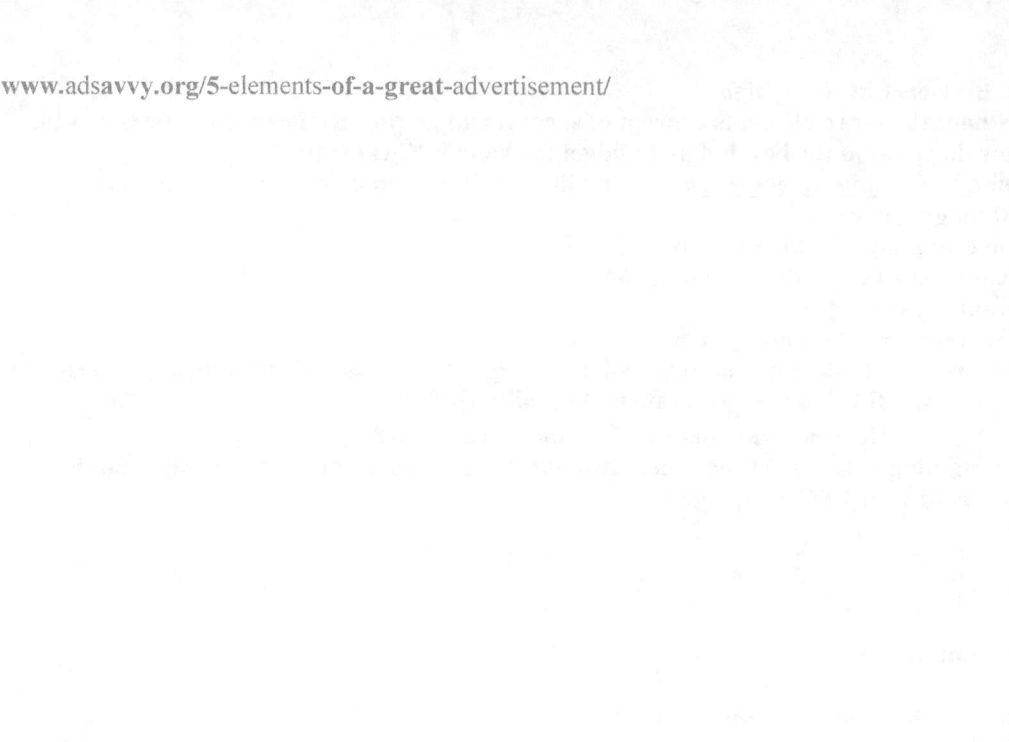

Intro to Lesson Two

So you want to be noticed for your new poster or web site ad. Advertising Design and the elements that make a successful design are important for you to review and to understand before you even begin to attempt to take the world by storm with your brilliant ad campaign. Here is a rather lengthy lesson plan outline (it might be wise to break it up into two lessons, actually) that examines some of the basics for practically every detail of your proposed ad. May the Force be With You.

Lesson 2 - Advertising Design

NOTICE THIS AD!

13. Advertising Design: Attention Is Always First

This one is simple. If people don't notice your ad, your chance of success is exactly zero. Your advertising design absolutely must get attention first.

Research indicates that 85% of ads don't get looked at, no matter how much they cost to produce. You have to be seen if you want action. Just imagine losing 85% of your customers because your ad doesn't stand out from the crowd. [Or think about increasing the response to your ads by SIX times before they do get noticed].

14. Advertising Design: Imagery

Strong imagery is the best attention getter. A picture is truly worth 1,000 words when it comes to getting attention. Ads that feature large visuals [60%-70% of the ad is the photo] score the highest for stopping power.

But you need to make sure that you get the right kind of attention. A big, beautiful, full color picture of a naked model will get you a lot of attention, but not the kind you want. Don't let a great picture dictate your advertising design. It is critical for your imagery to match your message. Your pictures have to match your copy, and together they must convey your intended message.

This is probably the most common mistake in advertising design. The pictures don't have much to do with the product or service, or they don't convey the right message. If the photo sells lust or humor, and you are selling security, the mental contrast will confuse all but the most determined readers. People will pass you by because the reason they were attracted to your ad [the picture] does not match what you are selling. You have attracted the wrong attention with your advertising design.

15. Advertising Design: Contrast

If imagery is the first way to get attention with your advertising design, then contrast is definitely the second way. Your ad must contrast with the other ads on the page. That is why it is critical for designers to see the actual medium you will be advertising in. If your ad just blends in with everything else on the page, you are wasting your money. If your graphic designer doesn't care where your ad appears – fire him or her.

Even worse than blending in, your customers might mistake your ad for your competitor's ad. You want your advertising design to give your company a unique look that contrasts with the other ads around it.

16. Advertising Design: Be Different

If imagery is first, and contrast is second, then being different is the third way to get attention with your advertising design.

People are attracted to unusual, new, funny, different things. You need to push your advertising design as far away from your conservative side as your willpower will let you. It may be hard, but do not listen to that little voice in your head telling you to do a quiet, calm, conservative ad. This is about results. Get a little crazy with your advertising design.

If you live in North America, then you have seen the very best advertising in the world. Americans are subject to the highest quality advertising ever created – every day. Judge your own advertising design by the absolutely brutal competition that you face. Your ads must come out on top. Professional Advertising is about getting results, and being a little different is definitely part of the formula.

17. How Many Customers Do You Really Need?
This question may seem odd coming from us, but we are serious. This is about maximizing your advertising dollar. Do you really need to reach everybody, or just enough people to keep your business growing stronger every year?
At advertising design agencies, it is often said that the best work ends up on the cutting room floor. Businesses often want their ads to be on the conservative side. Not too loud, not too risky. Loud, attention-getting ads are cut. But there is a tradeoff made with this decision.

18. Conservative ads don't get attention. They are conservative. They will, in the long run, make your business look highly professional and traditional. But the conservative strategy of advertising design is about the most expensive path you can choose.
Do you really need to be thought of as conservative? Even IBM now has dress-down Fridays. Dell computer uses a loud teenage spokesperson. Merrill Lynch uses a bull in a china shop. Maybe, [maybe], if you are a bank, a hospital, a non-profit, or a funeral home, conservative advertising design is the way to go. But conservative ads don't get attention.

And you need attention.

We are not endorsing risky advertising design here. But ask yourself, how many customers do I need? If my loud-happy-funny-sexy-strange-bright-weird shaped-purple and pink ad gets the attention of half of the people out there, maybe that's all I need. If you leave some of the conservative people behind with your advertising design, that's OK.
By getting attention with your advertising design, you will maximize your advertising dollar. Conservative advertising is very, very expensive. Don't go crazy, and always keep your target market in mind, but stretch to get attention with your advertising design. S-T-R-E-T-C-H to get ATTENTION!

19. Advertising Design: Using Photos and Illustrations
This one is also easy. Pay for the best, most appropriate photo or illustration available. Buy it, own it, keep it, and use it forever. Maybe it costs $100, or even $300. It is absolutely worth it.
There is an endless supply of fantastic photos available to you. There is a perfect photo out there for your business. Databases have tens of millions of super high quality photographs and illustrations. Find the right one that conveys your message, and you are half way to a highly effective ad.
Alternatively, if you use a poor photo, you have just cut the effectiveness of your advertising design in half. Remember, companies that cut corners on advertising design production are wasting a huge percentage of their advertising budget. Pay for high quality production up front, and use it forever. The cost of production is trivial in comparison to the cost of the media. Don't waste your money by skimping on good advertising design.
And of course there is a question of photo reproduction quality in the media you choose. Every newspaper is printed on a different type of press. Every press is different, and every printer is different. It's your designer's job to know how to get the best quality photo

reproduction from the specific press that is being used. You don't want your photos to look like mud in the newspaper.

20. Advertising Design: The Psychology Of Color In Advertising

Understanding how your customers interpret color in your advertising can be very important. First, different cultures interpret colors in different ways. Yellow represents jealousy in France, sadness in Greece, happiness in the United States, and is sacred in China. The moral, of course, is know your target audience.

Red is for excitement in advertising design. It is commonly used for automobile and food advertising. Red is passion and sex, danger, velocity, and power.

Yellow is a great attention grabber in advertising design. It is sunshine, warmth, and happiness. It is the first color your eye processes.

Blue represents reliability, trust, security, and technology. This is why businesses often use blue, green, teal, or gray in their advertising. Blue is also coolness and belonging.

Black represents sophistication and strength. It is elegant and seductive. For the right product, black is a great color.

Green is a cool, fresh color. It is nature and spring.

Purple is royalty. It is dignified and refined.

Pink is soft and feminine. It is security and sweetness.

White (white) is for cleanliness and purity in advertising design. It is youthful. But that doesn't mean it is for young people. Young people [teen and tween] prefer more trendy colors, like mauve and teal.

There is also white space to consider in advertising design. Without white space, you can't read the text. Photos lose their impact, and the ad loses balance. White space may be the most important component of your advertising design.

Gold is expensive and high class.

Orange is playful. It is autumn leaves, warmth and vibrancy.

Silver is prestigious. It represents cold and science.

Don't forget that every season has its' own colors, and fashion changes [every few minutes]. If you are trying to be trendy with your advertising design, then you have to keep up with the trends.

Is all of this important? Everything in advertising design is important.

When color is used correctly, it adds impact and clarity to your message. When color is used incorrectly, it can compromise your message and confuse your target audience.

Color can draw attention, lead the eye, and add emphasis. It can be used to show continuation and relatedness, or it can differentiate. Color certainly generates emotions and associations. Color has meaning for people, and you need to make sure that your colors say the right thing to your customers. Don't let poor advertising design destroy your marketing campaign.

Here's a quick example. In finance, the color red means loss. In engineering, it means hot or danger. In the medical field, it means danger or emergency or health. You want to make sure that you don't send the wrong message by using the wrong color. A high quality graphic designer will know the difference.

Advertising Design: The Elements Of Design

The elements of advertising design are the components of an advertisement that the graphic designer plans. The following list will help you to better understand what you graphic artist is talking about.

Color - Colors are considered in terms of intensity and brightness. As seen above, how color is used in your advertising design can have a big impact on how it is interpreted by your customers.

Value - Value describes the lightness or darkness of a color.

Line - A line is exactly what you think it is – a continuous mark connecting two points.

Shape - Shapes are two dimensional, or flat. A shape is height and width only in advertising design.

Form - Forms are three dimensional – height, width, and depth. You get volume and mass with form.

Texture - Texture describes the surface of an object. The artist renders the object to give an idea of how it would feel to the touch.

Space - In advertising design, space describes the distance between and around objects.

Balance - Balance describes the equality of objects in your ad. With symmetrical balance, both sides of your ad are the same. With asymmetrical balance, each side is different but equal. Radial balance means the ad is balanced around a focal point.

Contrast - Contrast describes the degree of difference between objects. It gets attention and adds excitement.

Emphasis - Emphasis and contrast are really the same thing in advertising design. The artist creates a focal or emphasis point in your ad by making it contrast with the other parts of the ad.

Proportion - Proportion describes how the individual elements of your ad relate to each other and to the entire piece.

Pattern - A pattern is exactly what you think it is – something repeated over and over again.

Rhythm - Rhythm gives your advertising design the feeling of movement or action. The artist places objects or creates patterns so that the eye follows a path. The path the eye follows in advertising is very important, because you want the reader to end up at your call for action [like at your phone number]. If the reader's eye stops at the wrong place in the ad, your call for immediate action may be seen too soon, or not at all.

Unity - Unity describes how the whole advertisement works together as a complete unit.

Variety - Variety describes the complexity of a work. In advertising, especially direct mail, a large amount of variety keeps the reader engaged and involved with the piece. The longer the reader is engaged, the better the odds of delivering your message are. That's why some ads are rather busy – they keep the reader involved.

ICA and HW 2

Answer the following essay questions

1. Why is getting your ad noticed important in advertising?
2. Why are colors important in advertising?
3. Why is advertising design important in advertising?
4. Why is spacing important in advertising?

Additional Internet Resources for this Lesson:

General Resource

http://www.askmrmovies.com
A Star is Born (1954) This Janet Gaynor film is a classic on how to get "discovered"

Advertising Design
www.wisegeek.com/what-is-advertising-design.htm

Color in Advertising

library.thinkquest.org
Intro to Lesson Three

Now we enter the whimsical world of David Ogilvy and his extremely personal take on classic advertising. Mr. Ogilvy examines the purpose of advertising, the elements of advertising, and the purpose of these elements. As long as Lesson 2 was, this lesson is extremely short and can be tacked on the second part of Lesson 2. However, just because Ogilvy is brief does not mean he is not profound in his incisiveness. Try to give each of his short instructions your fullest attention; you will be rewarded if you do.

Lesson 3 - The Purpose of Advertising

Advertising Elements	Element Purpose
1. Headline	Gets attention
2. Promises benefits	Builds interest
3. Pictures the outcome of benefits	Builds interest
4. Shows proof	Builds desire

5.	Differentiates	Builds desire
6.	Makes an offer	Builds desire
7.	Calls for action	Causes action

Example of a one page web advertisement with all of these elements done well:

http://bellagenix.com

1.   Headline – Look 10 Years Younger! – Gets attention from almost every woman over 30
2.   Promises Benefits – Tightens and Firms Skin, Reduces Wrinkles, Improves Skin Clarity! – Builds interest in almost every woman over 30
3.   Pictures the Outcome of Benefits – Before and After Photos With Dramatic Results – Builds interest in almost every woman over 30
4.   Shows Proof – Doctor Recommendation, Testimonials – Creates Desire in almost every woman over 30
5.   Differentiates – Discusses Expensive Botox Treatments as Costly Alternative – Creates More Desire in almost every woman over 30
6.   Makes an Offer – Yes! Send My Bottle Today! Click button! – By this time Desire is at a fever pitch and almost every woman over 30 cannot wait to press the button.
7.   Call For Action -Filling Out the Order Coupon – First Encounter With Hefty Price for 30 day supply (a bit over a dollar a day). Some desire lost here because of steep price, but a significant number of women over 30 will order this product regardless of price. – Causes Order to Proceed and Credit Card to be billed.

Another $35 for bellagenix. They did it right. They will make a lot of money. Will your ad be as good as this? This ad is a fine model to copy for numerous products. But do not copy the actual pictures or text; just copy the ELEMENTS OF ADVERTISING IN THE AD!

Popular Bromides from Ogilvy:

1.   *When people aren't having fun, they generally are not producing good work*
2.   *People are more productive when they imbibe a little alcohol*
3.   *Pay people peanuts and you will get monkeys*
4.   *99% of all advertising doesn't sell anything to anyone*
5.   *Don't keep a dog and bark yourself*
6.   *Hire people who are better than you*
7.   *You can't save souls in an empty church*
8.   *Don't bunt; try to hit one out of the park*

9.   *Coupons should be on the bottom right of a page* (This has proven to be incorrect)- Harvard Business School and Wharton School of Business at Penn suggest top center) The ad example above has its ad top right, so we can see a full picture of a woman with beautiful skin. To have the coupon in top center would interfere with that outstanding photo. So, use top right or top center according to the size of your photo.

10. *Orally, the best results are achieved at about 200 words a minute.* (This has also been refuted by the same two MBA programs above. 100 words a minute seems to be optimum according to their research.)

ICA and HW 3

Answer the following essays

1.   Discuss the various advertising elements and the purposes of those elements
2.   What does Ogilvy mean by saying you can't save souls in an empty church?
3.   What does Ogilvy mean by saying don't keep a dog and bark yourself?
4.   What does Ogilvy mean by saying pay people peanuts and you will get monkeys?
5.   What does Ogilvy mean by saying when people aren't having fun, they generally are not producing good work?

Additional Internet Resources for this Lesson:

General Resource
http://www.askmrmovies.com

Scientology (2012) – This scary John Philip Seymour tour-de-force performance is well worth watching to see how the media can be manipulated.

Wag the Dog (1997) – Another good film on media manipulation with Hoffman and DeNiro.

Purposes of Advertising

advertising.blurtit.com/q863338.html

www.mastersinadvertising.org/7-myths-and-facts-about-a-car

Intro to Lesson Four

As the manager of one of the most successful ad agencies in the history of Madison Avenue, Ogilvy is more than qualified to give the suggestions on the following lesson plan outline on how to manage your agency. You need not follow every suggestion, but you will certainly profit by following the majority of these time-tested principles.

Lesson 4 – How to Manage An Advertising Agency

Bromides by Ogilvy:

1.   Create a pleasant atmosphere for people to work in. Eliminate as much bureaucracy as possible and try to keep the network tight.
2.   Treat subordinates as human beings; help them when they encounter any type of difficulty on or off the job.
3.   Develop the talents of every worker in your organization to the maximum. Allow for failure and growth.
4.   Try to avoid top-down management. Group decisions are almost always better than one person's lone perspective.
5.   Have gentle manners and a degree of civility. Try not to be loud, boastful or obnoxious.
6.   Be as honest as possible with clients and with co-workers.
7.   Work hard, be objective and thorough.
8.   Avoid office politics, toadism, bullying, pompous behavior and ruthlessness
9.   Character matters for promotion.

10. When recommending a sales campaign to a client, act as if it were your own business
11. Be creative. Try not to copy other successful ad campaigns. Those campaigns became successful because they did not copy other ad campaigns.
12. Allow your client the right to disagree with you on how money should be spent
13. Company or corporate culture behavior should be the same in each country
14. Be aware of the mores of the country in which you are selling
15. Be discreet with ad campaigns and give full credit to the company; not the ad campaign
16. Avoid academic jargon as much as possible; keep things in simple language
17. Don't insult the intelligence of the consumer
18. Learn Direct Response Advertising before delving into other areas of advertising
19. Cutting prices as an ad inducement should always be a last resort
20. Cherish the Brand and forget quick fixes

ICA and HW 4

Answer the following essays:

1. What does Olgivy have to say about Brands?
2. How important is the art of learning Direct Response Advertising
3. Why is creativity so important in Advertising?
4. Why should you treat your client as if it were you own company?
5. Why is honesty the best policy both in the office and with clients?

Additional Internet Resources for this Lesson:

General Resource

http://www.askmrmovies.com

The Hucksters (1947) Gable movie hits the spot about honesty in ads

Branding
marketing.about.com

Creativity in Advertising
muse.jhu.edu/journals/asr/v008/8.4unit15.html

Intro to Lesson Five

Ogilvy had a special appreciation of the art of Direct Mail. He firmly believed that the ad people in Direct Mail were the best writers in the business of advertising and his numerous successful campaigns utilizing the basic principles of good Direct Mail copywriting proved his point over and over again. Ignore these nuggets of wisdom suggested by Blair Entenmann at your own peril. You can easily convert these principles of direct mail to email as well.

Lesson 5 – How to Get Clients – Direct Mail

The Principles of Targeted Direct Mail Advertising
By Blair Entenmann, President of Marketing Help!

Advertising does work. It not only creates a better, more productive selling environment, but properly done, can generate inquiries and sales! If you can identify your ideal customer, you should use targeted direct mail. When you spend hard-earned dollars on direct mail, you want it to be noticed, not forgotten. The objective for direct mail is Open Me, Read Me, Call Me Today! The following principles can make your direct mail more productive and deliver exceptional results!

1. Mail to the Right Prospect with Frequency. Two-thirds of direct mail's success is in the mailing list - the better the list, the better the results. Invest the time and money into finding or building a mailing list of prospects who would be interested in your product or service. Consider a two- or three- part direct mail campaign. Timing may be a critical success factor - today they aren't interested, but next month they might be. Repetition will

generate a better response. A general rule is that it takes 6-9 advertising or sales contacts before a suspect buys.

2. Make It Stand Out. What attention-getting, fun and creative device can you use that has some linkage to your product or service? Be different in size, shape, and color than competitor's mailings, such as a large square envelope, a bright yellow envelope, or triangular mailing tube. Use postcards, greeting cards, or even frisbees to deliver your message. What attention-getting words work best for your prospects? Words like Free, New, Now, Breakthrough, Finally, and Limited Time are powerful, magic words that can evoke a positive response. A good creative concept, combined attention-getting graphics and copy will make your direct mail noticeable.

3. Make It Interesting. Make an offer so good that your customers simply can't refuse. Find out what they want and offer it to them. Use benefit-oriented customer promises for headlines such as "Prevent Theft of Your Valuables" or "Reduce Your Warranty Costs With Quality Components!" Write selling copy about what theprospect wants to know in clear, concise sentences. Adding a powerful cover letter to a great brochure can increase your response. A letter allows you to reveal and customize a major promotional offer or get the prospect involved in your product or service. Personalized laser letters (Dear Blair) are more effective than form letters (Dear Sportsman). Use headlines within the letter to summarize the benefit of the following paragraph. Can you include an advertising specialty that could enhance the prospect's curiosity?

4. TEST, TEST, TEST. Run two different campaigns or promotions at the same time (i.e A/B Test) to see which performs better. Then run the winner with the other half of your prospect list against the next big idea. Overtime you will improve your results based on what your prospects/new customers want.

5. Make It Easy to Respond NOW. Ask for the response you would like and help them do it. Your direct mail piece is your salesperson and it should ask for the order! In sales letters, use a P.S. to make a strong call to action. Use a business reply card, 800- number, fax number, or web site that offers a one step process. Give an incentive for the desired response (i.e. free gift or special consideration if you act now). Your response rate will be higher if you give customers several ways to respond.

6. Track Your Results. Create a tracking system so you can determine what works and what doesn't. Analyze your results on a Cost Per Inquiry, Cost Per Proposal/Estimate/Appointment and Cost per Sale basis. Sometimes a low response promotion offer has sky high sales conversion, making it a more profitable sale than a high response, low sales conversion promotion offer.

ICA and HW 5

Answer the following essays

1. Why should you create a mailing list?
2. Why should you carefully track your sales results every time you run a new ad?
3. Why should you continually test your ad campaign?
4. What are the advantages and disadvantages of direct mail?

Additional Internet Resources for this Lesson:

General Resource

http://www.askmrmovies.com

use the link below on how to give effective email campaigns

http://unbounce.com/email-marketing/the-6-point-guide-to-an-irresistible-email-teaser-campaign/

Direct Mail Advertising

www.alladvertisingagencies.com

Direct Mail Response

www.dmnews.com

Intro to Lesson Seven

Ogilvy knew there was more than one way to cook eggs and have people enjoy each dish; regardless of how you cooked them. The point was to prepare them well. Ogilvy, of course, was a world class chef before he became an ad man on Madison Avenue, so he knew a little bit about preparing dishes or ad campaigns in different ways. This lesson plan outline looks at some of his recipes for success.

Lesson 6 - Methods of Client Recruitment

    A. Direct Mail as explained in the previous lesson
    B. When negotiating with clients directly, emphasize quality over quantity. Better to have one good copywriter on an account than six mediocre ones.
    C. Never underestimate the power of creativity from either a client standpoint or from the standpoint of the agency.
    D. Creative energy is another important variable in the ad process. Merely having a good idea does not get the job done unless you have creative energy to see the idea to fruition.
    E. A simple proposition like "if our campaign does not increase your sales, then you will not be billed" goes a long way to recruiting new clients for your base.
    F. Show potential clients that you can do the following without difficulty: define problems and opportunities for the client, set up short and long-range goals for the client with measurable results (usually sales), be able to lead large groups of

executives, make lucid presentations to committees, and be able to operate within the parameters of a client's budget.

G.   There are currently over 10,000 advertising agencies; how will you differentiate yourself from the others?

H.   Make contacts and friends with news agencies, TV stations, radio stations and every media you can think of. Take them out to lunch and let them know about your agency and the services it offers.

I.   As you make more money, it is suggested that you begin to upgrade your clients. Your clients will be starkly aware of the status of your other clients. The bottom 3000 agencies will take anyone as a client, the next level of agencies will have minimal standards for clients, the final 3000 agencies will only handle the upper end of clients, and the top 1000 agencies (and hopefully, your agency) will handle only the companies that make the most money.

J.   Free presentations are known as speculative presentations in the advertising business. But in addition to a speculative presentation, one must offer the "sales will increase or there will be no charge for the advertising campaign". The odds of a client's sales going up under ANY campaign for three months is approximately 81%, so that almost anything you do will result in a profit for the client. However, if there are SUBSTANTIAL increases in sales, it may be a result of your creative advertising campaign.

K.   There has to be a genuine chemistry between the client and the agency or the campaign will have more difficulty than most other campaigns.

L.   EXTENSIVE RESEARCH IS ABSOLUTELY MANDATORY FOR THE SUCCESS OF ANY ADVERTISING CAMPAIGN. EVERY AGENT SHOULD BE ABLE TO CITE THE RESEACH DONE BEFORE MEETING WITH A POTENTIAL CLIENT.

ICA and HW 6

Answer the following essays:

1.   Why is quality more important than quantity in advertising?
2.   Why is creativity an important factor in advertising?
3.   Why should you try to create a niche for your agency?
4.   Why should you sometimes give free or speculative presentations to potential clients?
5.   Why is research one of the most essential parts of your presentation?

Additional Internet Resources for this Lesson:

General Resource

http://www.askmrmovies.com

check this resource for presentations
http://www.cinemacon.com/

The Importance of Research in Advertising

http://en.wikipedia.org/wiki/Advertising_research

How to Give Excellent Presentations

http://www.forbes.com/fdc/welcome_mjx.shtml
Intro to Lesson Seven

We leave the optimistic world of Ogilvy for one lesson to plant our feet in the realities of entry-level jobs in the advertising business. Being successful at an entry-level job at a good advertising agency is akin to crossing Fifth Avenue fifty times during rush hour without having a close call with a vehicle. Of course, if you are outside of New York, things are a bit easier. And if you are in China, chances are you are about the only one in your office, or even in your whole company who knows anything about professional advertising.

Lesson 7 – The Harsh Realities of Entry-Level Jobs in Advertising

    A. There is only one reason for any company in the world to hire you for anything; that would be to make more money for the company.
    B. Generally speaking, most companies view sales as a barometer of your success; the more sales you are responsible for, the more money you will make at any level in the job market.
    C. Just like 90% of all businesses fail within three years, 90%+ of all entry-level workers fail at their jobs within three years. Just do the math. If 90% of all companies fail, then 90% of all the sales "professionals" must be failing as well.
    D. An entry-level worker in sales can, at times, be an immediate success. There is no timetable to success in sales; just increased sales.
    E. You can be the hardest worker in the office who puts in 100 hours a week, is a fine, upstanding family man, honest, sincere and loyal and if your sales numbers are not up in a very short time (usually three months), you will be canned.

23

F.   You can be the laziest worker in the office who is always late, takes off lots of sick days, fools around with every woman in the office, be dishonest, insincere, disloyal, a liar, thief and pervert, play games on your computer all day and leave work early and still get a big raise and promotion if your sales numbers are up. Be sure to compare E and F the next time somebody utters the silly phrase "but that's not fair!"

G.   A good ad does not guarantee increased sales, but it does give you a better opportunity to succeed at getting more sales. Like most other things in life, there are no guarantees in a business career. In general terms, an ad or promo is only good if it increases sales.

H.   Getting the job is primarily dependent on convincing the Human Resources clerk that you are a team player and would like to prove yourself to be an asset to the team to increase sales for the company. Stressing your independence, new ways of thinking, individual accomplishments and qualities, and desire to have your own company one day, will only insure that you will not get the job. Hiding all of these desires and sublimating them to the needs of a team player for the company will go a lot further for your chances of being hired.

ICA and HW 7

Answer the following essays

1.   How are humans similar to most companies?
2.   How are entry-level sales people judged by their employer?
3.   How long does it usually take for a new salesperson to be successful in their new job?
4.   How important is a good ad to your sales campaign? And how is a good ad measured?
5.   Why is it more important to show how much of a team player you are in your initial interview than being an independent thinker or person with great individual accomplishments?

Additional Internet Resources for this Lesson:

General Resource

Commercial Man (2001)

Entry-Level Advertising Jobs

Reward Systems For Advertising Executives

Intro to Lesson Eight

Here is another practical lesson plan outline that describes some of the dos and don'ts of moving up the ladder in advertising. It may be worth your while to pay very close attention to each part of this section. People who work hard in advertising are not worth as much to the company as people who create more revenue; it is as simple as that.

Lesson 8 – Moving Up the Ladder to the Next Level in Advertising

A.   Okay, let's say you got lucky in your first three to six months and put up increasing numbers in sales for your team. Trust me when I tell you that you have already been noticed. If you are truly a force to be reckoned with, and your sales manager thinks you can handle the job, you might be offered an assistant sales manager's position in as little as six months on the job. This is good news and bad news.

B.   The good news is that you will have a title, possibly your own office space, and a bit more money and power.

C.   The bad news is that your sales manager will most likely be taking credit for most of your ideas, campaigns and sales increases. He or she will be gunning for the next rung on the ladder, which is regional sales manager or manager of a larger territory. You will not be getting an offer for the regional position, even if you are the prime reason that sales have increased.

D.   You will most likely be doing all the work of the sales manager while he or she is sniffing around for a better job. In reality, you will actually be the new sales manager. You will now be responsible for doing all of the duties of a sales manager, which include, but are not limited, to the following: 1. Hiring new sales people, 2. Firing current ineffective sales people, 3. Closely monitoring the sales numbers of your current team, 4. Creating new sales campaigns, such as the ones in the film *Glengary Glenross* (see review at askmrmovies.com) "First Place is a brand new car, Second Place is a new set of steak knives and Third Place is your fired" This type of competition is usually set up every month. A typical sales team of six may compete for the two "prizes" with the lowest two performers almost being certain to be fired. The next two above them will, most likely, be put on a type of "probation" for a month, which, when translated, means that they will be fired the next month if they don't finish either first or second in sales.
E.   Exceptions to the survival of the fittest scenario in D are if the entire sales force is relatively bunched up closely in sales numbers, but everyone is turning in acceptable numbers. Remember, however, that acceptable numbers is a relative term. 100,000 in sales in one month might be acceptable, while in another month could possibly mean you would be fired.
F.   You success as an assistant Sales Manager is closely tied to the results of your sales team, so it is essential that you formulate the team you want and try to ensure their success to the highest degree. If they fail, you will not only lose your position of Assistant Sales Manager; you might get canned completely from the company. Most of the time, however, the worst that will happen to you is that you get thrown back into the pack of general sales people. This is also the time to try out, and take credit for, some new ad campaigns that you think might work.

ICA and HW 8

Answer the following essays:

1.   When will you be promoted from salesperson to Assistant Sales Manager?
2.   What is the good news and bad news of becoming a new Assistant Sales Manager?
3.   What, in general, are the new responsibilities of an Assistant Sales Manager?
4.   What are "acceptable numbers"?
5.   Why is putting together your sales team and ensuring their success so important to your own success?
6.   What will happen if your sales team fails?

Additional Internet Resources for this Lesson:

Film Resource
Glengarry Glenross

http://www.askmrmovies.com

Duties of an Assistant Sales Manager

http://education-
portal.com/articles/Advertising_Manager_Job_Description_and_Requirements_for_a
_Career_in_Advertising_Management.html

How to Hire and Fire Salespeople Effectively

http://www.rabinsite.org/academyLms/content/workbooks/mc2workbook.pdf
 Intro to Lesson Nine

   Here is some good general advice on how to present yourself to your supervisors and co-workers; whether it be in the West or in China. This lesson plan outline examines advertising ethics (yes, good advertising agencies DO have good ethics) and you need to understand them.

Lesson 9 – Ethics and the Workplace Socialization Trap

   A.   Socializing in the workplace (and particularly in the SALES workplace) can be extremely hazardous to your employment health. Men and women have slept with each other just to get ahold of sales leads. A fight between dating salespeople can be poisonous for the entire sales team. Be wary of any romantic overtures in your sales office. There are plenty of other places to meet people of the opposite sex. Despite promoting teamwork and closeness within the group, there is always that distance created by competition for the top two slots in the office lurking behind every smile, every drink or celebration and every social situation in the office.
   B.   If you are married, you are extremely vulnerable if you try to date someone in the office. Everyone knows you are married. Everyone knows you are fooling around. All it takes is one enemy to bring you down and your career at that company is over. Does this happen often in many companies? Of course it does. Do some people get away with it? Of course they do. But you won't/ because the odds are stacked very high against you. Some even say that sex with their wife is much better the sex they get outside the house. If that is true, then why have hamburger when you can have steak at home?
   C.   Teambuilding is one thing; getting too chummy with your co-workers on business trips in another thing altogether. It happens quite often and the results

are favoritism, group disenchantment, falling sales and eventual dismissal from your sales manager position.

D.   Never forget for one second that the bottom line in all businesses is profit from sales. Everything else is an illusion or irrelevant. You CAN have one or more girlfriends outside of your home. You can have as many affairs as you like and the company will even pay for them PROVIDED your sales figures continue to go up. Morals and ethics have never been the long suit of advertising, sales and prosperous companies. Cheating on your wife or husband, however, gives your competition (both inside and outside the office) an edge they would not normally have. Why give the competition an edge?

E.   On RARE occasions, a genuine office romance will blossom between two unattached members of the opposite sex and this is all well and good. However, never forget for a minute that many ruthless companies consider married women a liability because they can become pregnant at a moment's notice and lose valuable company time for sales and profits because of their inability to keep up with single males who have no responsibilities whatsoever. Despite laws to the contrary, many companies hire only single men and women dedicated to their jobs. They will also hire married men without children. This bias of the worst type is commonly practiced by innumerable sales departments. Once again, though, you can be a woman who is pregnant, have six children and two boyfriends in the office as long as your sales figures continue to climb.

F.   Softball teams, bowling teams, golf teams, tennis teams and other company teams are a good idea for sales morale. Parties, going to a bar after work, or going to someone's apartment from work may not be the wisest choice for most workers. Some might say they might lose their jobs if they don't socialize and go drinking "with the guys". News flash; the only thing that counts is your sales; nothing else matters. Come up with a better ad.

ICA and HW 9

Answer the following essays:

1.   Why is socializing in the sales and advertising workplace sometimes a dangerous activity?
2.   Why do married people sometimes have difficulty in the sales and advertising workplace?
3.   Why are sales conventions and business trips sometimes a dangerous situation?
4.   Why are sales ultimately the only thing that counts as far as ethics are concerned in most companies?
5.   Why are women at a disadvantage in the sales and advertising workplace?
6.   Why are company team activities preferable to parties and going for a drink after work?

Additional Internet Resources for this Lesson:

Film Resource
Madmen (any episode)

http://www.askmrmovies.com

Challenges of Women in the Sales and Advertising Workplace

http://www.blastradius.com/ideas/confessions-of-a-female-exec/

(It seems the author like David Ogilvy's title so much, she used it for her own book)

Team-building in Sales

http://www.teambuildingproductions.net/commercials.htm

Intro to Lesson Ten

In Lesson Ten's outline, we examine the joys of getting your first account. Then, we examine the panic that sets in once you realize that you will most likely be fired if you are not successful with this account. Read on for your first thrill of success or your first failure in the business with many more of each emotion to follow in the future. If you want security, get a job at a bank or a school (of course, you will not make nearly as much money).

Lesson 10 – Your First Account

A.   **Congratulations. You just landed your first advertising account. You may have been an assistant for months before they gave you your own or maybe you got lucky and started off with one as soon as you were hired. Either way, you can bet the ranch that the account you were given is extremely unimportant. They are not going to trust a major account to a junior advertising agent. This is good news and bad news. The good news is you have your first account and a chance to show what you can do. The bad news is that it is probably an account that no other senior member wanted and that anyone in the office longer than you had already passed on. Chances that you will fail with this account are very high; well over 50%. However, you probably won't get fired if you fail, because no one wanted it in the first place. It is probably a very difficult item to sell or make attractive to the public. Let me give you an example; Ace Bug Spray for Cockroaches.**
B.   **How do you make a toxic bug spray attractive? Let's face it, bug spray is not very attractive, so you have to attack the problem from a different perspective; how much do people hate cockroaches? Can you tap into the psychological fear element of cockroaches in the kitchen, bathroom and bedroom? I had a group of students work on this account and this is what they came up with. One student had a man wake up with a gigantic cockroach in bed with him instead of his wife. This student went for the humorous angle. Another student had a group of**

cockroaches raiding the refrigerator, leaving no food for the family. This was also a humorous approach. A third student has a man ask his wife to pass him the towel after he has showered and a cockroach hands him a towel. So my best students thought that humor was the best way to handle this product and I agree with them.

C.   How do you beat the competition? They say that truth is the first casualty of war. Well, that is also true in advertising. Every product claims to be the best and least expensive. Of course, that is not mathematically likely, but they all claim it, anyway. So your product must automatically be the best on the market (even if it isn't) . The next question is why is it the best on the market? Now you have to come up with a reasonable idea why it is the best. One of my students used this ploy: "Other sprays are used and the bugs keep coming back, but Ace Bug Spray works after just one use (and the bugs will be back after this one use as well). Notice the wording in the ad; it doesn't actually claim that the bugs will not come back after one use; it merely states that it WORKS after just one use. Well, all bug sprays work after one use, but that is not important. The reader THINKS that the bugs will not come back after one use. This is the power of suggestion.

Another student used the economic model for her ad; "Kills them dead with just ONE spray" The implication here is that you do not need a lot of the product to get rid of your problems, so that in the long run, you will save money. Actually, all bug sprays kill any bug with just one spray, but no other company thought of making that a slogan. This is how you beat the competition. Be aware that you are already on slippery ice in the ethical arena.

D.   The Artwork and Copy should be graphic and send a message to the buyer. Show a dead bug and the words "just one spray, and they go away" one student submitted. All bugs go away after one spray, but the idea the picture gives is that the spray kills the bug and no other bugs will ever come near there again (what a fantasy). The face of the bug should be in agony or in fear. In reality, bugs do not have facial expressions of either. Show a woman on the can killing the bug. Most women hate bugs and are cleaner more than most men (who are generally dirty pigs who don't care if a few bugs are in the house). The can is a weapon in the hands of the woman and empowers her to a degree.

E.   Get your product known and distributed. You can't increase sales by waiting for customers to come to you. The ad exec handling this account will have to become involved in the marketing and distribution of this product as well as getting involved from the creative end. Literally splash the internet with your product. Have a sale; 33% off. Buy two and get one free (the same as a 33% off sale). Contact stores in poor neighborhoods; they have the most houses with cockroaches. Target poor and working- class people; they are the ones who suffer the most from these little critters. Find out what your competition is charging and meet or beat the price.

F.   Congratulations. Your market share is up 1% this month. The ad campaign was a success. The Ace Bug Spray company made an extra $200,000 in sales. They will be very happy to give your ad agency a $10,000 bonus on top of the $10,000 they paid for the campaign. Your first ad campaign was a success, but don't let that go to your head. You could have just as easily have failed. Sooner or later, one of your ad campaigns will fail. This is a mathematical certainty. But enjoy your first success. If you had failed, you would have to ignore your failure and come up with a better campaign the next time.

ICA and HW 10

Answer the following essays

1.   Why is it good news and bad news to get your first account in an ad agency?
2.   How do you make bug spray attractive to the buyer?
3.   How do you beat your competition?
4.   Why are artwork and copy important?
5.   What should you do if you are successful with your first ad campaign? How should you handle failure?

Additional Internet Resources for this Lesson:

General Resource

http://www.askmrmovies.com

Lust For Life (1956) – Great artist film

First Accounts at Ad Agencies

http://en.wikipedia.org/wiki/Account_planning

Artwork and Copy on Ad Campaigns

http://www.rottentomatoes.com/m/1216754-art_and_copy/ (documentary film)

Intro to Lesson Eleven

OK, so you got lucky and made a hit with your first campaign. That is both a good thing and not so good thing. Now that you were successful with one client, your managers will be expecting you to be successful with EVERY client. In baseball, you can make outs two out of three times, and still lead the league in hitting, but in advertising, that would only get you fired. Check out this lesson plan outline on how to add to your initial success.

Lesson 11 - Adding to Your Account Portfolio

A.   So you had a bit of success with your first client. Don't let it go to your head. There are only two directions you can go in business; either up or down. No one just glides along on what they have accomplished. You are either increasing sales for your agency or your sales are decreasing, which would mean, of course, you would eventually be asked to leave. Let's assume for the sake of argument you are on the uptrend. You were successful with Ace Bug Spray and now you have caught the eye of the senior partners of the firm and put fear into the heart of some of the other members of your agency. You might be in line for another account; this time it will be a bigger and/or better account than Ace Bug Spray. Maybe you will work with the "A" team instead of the "B" team. Whatever situation you find yourself in, you can bet the ranch it will be more complex than your first account. Be prepared for a larger client.

B.   Your company just laid off Bill Clemens, who had been with the firm for three years. It appears that Bill's streak of luck ended when he was given a solid account and let it go downhill for two straight quarters. Was Bill good or bad? Really doesn't matter. The only thing that matters is sales; and they were down two straight quarters. You have been handed the account. The good news is you

can probably fail with this assignment and still be retained, because then the agency will think there is something wrong with the client if two ad agents fail on a client in a row. (Clients will usually drop you anyway if they encounter two failures in a row as well). The bad news is that you turned around Ace Bug Spray and expectations are high that you will turn around the Alibaba Sneaker Company, which had great success for its first year on the American market (they come from China, naturally), but increased pressure from Nike and Adidas has reversed some of the gains they had made in market share in the first year. Your job is to increase their current market share of 4% to 5% or even the 6 % they had in the first year.

C.   Remember, you still have to service your other client, Ace Bug Spray, in addition to coming up with a campaign for Alibaba Sneakers. Be sure not to spread yourself too thin by taking too many clients at one time. Delegate some authority to one of your assistants (by this time, the senior members will have given you an assistant). Have them keep tabs on the Ace Bug Spray campaign to make sure it is progressing according to your expectations. Then you can begin to organize your new campaign for Alibaba Sneakers.

D.   So what went wrong with Alibaba Sneakers? Why did they lose market share for the last two quarters. You need to do extensive research before attempting your new campaign. Your research shows that Nike created a low-end product to compete with the low prices offered by Alibaba Sneakers. This reduced the advantage that Alibaba Sneakers had when they first hit the market and undersold all the other domestic sneaker brands. So Nike has attacked you. You need to attack Nike right back. One of my students was assigned the Alibaba Sneaker problem and came up with this solution; copy the top of the line styles of Nike and sell them for much less with all the same components. Use an independent consumer reports group to compare your top of the line styles and quality with that of Nike for the prices that both are offered for. The consumer group should come up with the conclusion that for the price, Alibaba Sneakers offer all the same quality that the top of the line Nike sneakers offer, but at a lower price. If you can accomplish this strategy, you will be in line for a very big bonus, a big raise, a new office and in line for even bigger and better accounts.

E.   What if you fail? What if Alibaba Sneakers does not want to take the chance of going head to head with the powerful Nike? Then you will either be fired or given another chance with another account. Regardless of the outcome, you will always have to create a new campaign with new ideas. Even if you work for half a dozen advertising agencies, all it takes is one good idea and one good campaign to make your mark in the advertising world. Just keep swinging away, and sooner or later, you will hit one out of the park.

ICA and HW 11

Answer the following essays:

1. What will happen if you have success with your first client?
2. What will happen if you fail to turn around a client with problems?
3. How should you service your clients if you add more clients to your portfolio?
4. How can you counterattack the competition?
5. How should you treat a failed advertising campaign?

Additional Internet Resources for this Lesson:

General Resource

http://www.askmrmovies.com

Failure: The Movie (2012)

Adding to Your Client Base

http://www.shmoop.com/careers/sales-representative/

Handling Failure in Advertising

http://www.theradiostations.com/12-causes-advertising-failure

Intro to Lesson Twelve

There is a saying that we are judged by the company we keep. Nothing is truer than that statement in the advertising world. If you sleep with pigs, you will be considered a pig yourself; regardless of your three-piece suit from Brooks Brothers. The following advice from Ogilvy should not only be followed, but followed to the letter.

Lesson 12 – How to Select Clients for Advertising

A.   Contrary to popular belief, a good advertising company does not take every client that come through the door. To do so would jeopardize the reputation of the agency you are trying to build.

B.   Be proud to advertise the product your client is trying to sell. If you have a problem selling lady's underwear, then don't accept the account.

C.   Never accept an account unless you think you can perform a verifiably better job than your predecessor.

D.   Try not to add clients with a long stretch of consecutive losses in market share over several quarters.

E.   Avoid clients who are too demanding; demanding clients often have preconceived notions of what works and what doesn't work. This stifles creativity and the ability of your staff to mount an effective new campaign.

F.   Seek out clients with products of low unit cost, universal use, and frequent purchase (toothbrushes, toilet paper, candy, drinks, etc). They have larger budgets and are easier to test than high-ticket items.

G.   Avoid groups or committees that require more than ONE person to okay your advertising campaign. Make sure you are accountable to the boss alone and no one else.

H.   Do not accept a client with a condition that you must have one of their workers on your staff.

I.   Avoid clients that act like bullies.

J.   Avoid clients that publically announce you as a candidate for their campaign. Public failure to recruit such a client results in damage to your agency.

K.   Avoid competing with more than three other agencies at any one time for an account.

ICA and HW 12

Answer the following essays:

      1.   **Why should you be selective in choosing clients to service for your agency?**
      2.   **Why should you avoid demanding clients?**
      3.   **Why should you seek out clients with products that have low unit cost?**
      4.   **Why should you avoid publically competing for a campaign?**
      5.   **Why should avoid situations where advertising campaigns need the approval of more than one person?**

Additional Internet Resources for this Lesson:

General Resource

http://www.askmrmovies.com

Erin Brockovich (2000) examines ethics in advertising

Criteria for Accepting New Clients in Advertising

http://www.ehow.com/info_8681316_procedures-new-accounts-advertising-company.html

Avoiding Improper Clients in an Advertising Agency

http://marketing.about.com/od/advertising/tp/marketmistakes.htm

Intro to Lesson Thirteen

Here Ogilvy advises us on how to keep clients. Getting them is sometimes easier than keeping them. Losing a client can be problematic for both you and your company. Be prepared for the eventual loss of a client by having a Plan B in case they leave your ship. Ogilvy gives us numerous tips on how to keep our clients happy.

Lesson 13 – How to Keep Clients

A. The average client changes advertising agencies every seven years. **Make sure you devote your best workers to MAINTAINING clients, not obtaining NEW ones. You should separate your company functions into Client Initiation and Client Maintenance. Never mix the two with one person.**

B. Know of the history of your client's advertising and their agencies; avoid clients that change agencies frequently or have a poor history with their agencies

C. When establishing a relationship with a client, try to establish communication at all levels of the company.

D. Try to deal with the highest level of the company at all times; CEOs and Presidents are less troublesome than dealing with subordinates.

E. Do not put too much emphasis on any single client. Having a disproportionate amount of business from one client can eventually lead to losing a disproportionate amount of business if you lose that client.

F. Measure the time required to service your client. Take the fee paid by your client and divide by the amount of hours spent on his or her account. If the average hourly payment falls below X, you should drop the client.

G. Avoid teams and committees whenever possible; make your presentation to the CEO, president or some other major decision-maker; not an underling.

H. Make sure you rehearse your presentation two or three times before you actually give it to your potential client.

I.   Avoid using committees or more than one person to give a presentation; research has shown one speaker is more effective than a group of speakers.

J.   Tell your client to the truth; even if you costs you the account.

K.   Do not allow bullying of any type within your office or agency; fire anyone who is not harmonious or, at the very least, cooperative and flexible.

ICA and HW 13

Answer the following essays:

1.   Why is maintaining clients just as important as obtaining them in the first place?

2.   Why should you thoroughly research the history of your potential client's advertising history?

3.   Why should you present to the highest level of your potential client's company?

4.   Why should you avoid any disproportionate contract from a potential client?

5.   How should you make a decision to drop a client?

6.   Why should you be truthful at all times with all your clients?

7.   Why should not allow bullying in your office or agency?

Additional Internet Resources for this Lesson:

General Resource

http://www.askmrmovies.com

Tucker (1988) – great presentation film

How to Retain Advertising Clients

http://www.marketingdonut.co.uk/marketing/customer-care/how-to-retain-customers-in-hard-times

Secrets to Good Presentations

http://www.thinkoutsidetheslide.com/ten-secrets-for-using-powerpoint-effectively/

Intro to Lesson Fourteen

It is important to realize that it takes two to tango in the advertising game. You cannot be successful without the cooperation of your client, and your client cannot be successful unless they cooperate with you. In this lesson plan outline, Ogilvy suggests how clients should behave toward their ad men or women.

Lesson 14 – How Should Clients Behave Toward Your Agency?

    A. Clients should not create an atmosphere of fear for your agency.
    B. To a substantial degree, client behavior determines the success or failure of a good advertising campaign.
    C. Allow your advertising agency to do the creative end of the work; do not compete with them in this area.
    D. Work directly with your agency as the head of your company.
    E. Make sure your advertising agency is well-paid for increasing your profits each quarter. You can bet you will penalize them or fire them if sales go down in any quarter, so be prepared to pay them well for success.

F.   Your agency's expenses are measured in HOURS; if you want additional research, pre-testing, test presentations, split advertising tests, tv spots, radio spots, newspapers spots, be prepared to pay for each of these additional services according to hourly billing fees. The hourly fee for each of these and other activities can vary, but should be negotiated in advance of contract.

G.   Be candid with your agency and have your agency be candid with you.

H.   Numbers generally don't lie; only people lie. If your numbers say it's time for a new ad campaign; follow the numbers. If your numbers are good, don't fix it if it ain't broke.

I.   Switch to MONTHLY plans from QUARTERLY plans. Better to find a turkey in one month or a great ad campaign in one month.

ICA and HW 14

Answer the following essays:

1.   Why should you not bully your advertising agency?

2.   Why should the creative end of the advertising campaign come from the agency?

3.   Why should you reward your advertising agency well for profitable months and quarters?

4.   Why should you be aware of the amount of hours your advertising agency will spend on your behalf?

5.   How should your company behave in relation to the numbers that come in every month or quarter?

6.   Why are monthly plans more effective than quarterly plans?

Additional Internet Resources for this Lesson:

General Resource

http://www.askmrmovies.com

Creativity: The Movie (isn't it great that you can learn to be creative from a movie? I have a bridge I would like to sell you as well in Brooklyn)

http://www.creativitymovie.com/

Creativity in Advertising

http://hbr.org/2013/06/creativity-in-advertising-when-it-works-and-when-it-doesnt/ar/1

Billing in Advertising

http://advertising.about.com/od/advertisingglossaryb/g/Billings.htm

Intro to Lesson Fifteen

Building a great ad campaign is not mostly luck (although there is some luck involved); it takes a great deal of research and hard work. Above all else, it takes discipline. This lesson plan outline examines Ogilvy's sound advice on how to build a solid ad campaign.

Lesson 15 – How to Build a Solid Ad Campaign

    A. Be highly disciplined with your plan and implementation
    B. There are four good advertisements:
        1. Any advertisement that the client oks (according to one school of thought)
        2. Any advertisement that is remembered by the public and the industry
        3. Any advertisement that sells without drawing attention to the advertisement, but only to the product
        4. Any advertisement that increases the sales of the previous quarter (author's opinion)
    C. Creativity can be overrated. More important than creativity are sales increases over the last quarter.
    D. Learn the REALITIES of advertising. Mail Order relies almost solely on advertising. One month is plenty of testing time for this process.
    E. Make a promise that is enticing to customers of the client and give the facts.
    F. Try to build your brand with your advertisements; this will increase your sales
    G. Avoid discounts and price off deals; they tend to cheapen your product
    H. Don't copy other successful commercials or advertisements; they work for other products, but might not work for yours.

Answer the following essays:

1. What are considered good advertisements?
2. Why is creativity overrated?
3. What is the importance of a promise to the consumer?
4. Why is building you brand important?
5. Why should you avoid discounts and coupons for your product?
6. Why is it advisable not to copy other advertisements?

Additional Internet Resources for this Lesson:

General Resource

http://www.askmrmovies.com

The Greatest Movie Ever Sold (documentary 2011) – Good film about branding

How to Build Brand

http://www.wikihow.com/Build-Brand-Equity

Creating a Promise for the Consumer

http://www.gazelles.com/columns/Brand%20Promise.pdf

Intro to Lesson Sixteen

This is where Ogilvy's expertise in Direct Mail comes to the fore. In this lesson plan outline, he takes us step by step through the world of Direct Mail ad copy writing; the essence of good advertising. These principles are rock-solid and are backed up with verifiable ad campaigns that have made millions of dollars, and can be easily practiced for email advertising. So take notice.

Lesson 16 – How to Write Excellent Copy

A.   The Headline is the most important part of your ad copy. 80% of your success or failure will depend on your headline.

B.   Two most powerful words in advertising are FREE and NEW.

C.   How to is another powerful advertising phrase.

D.   Longer Headlines of at LEAST 6-10 Words sell more than shorter Headlines.

E.   Include your selling promise in your headline if possible.

F.   Try to include the brand name in your headline. Avoid negatives in headlines.

G.   Body Copy is the text that is read under the Headline. Avoid analogies; even simple ones.

H.   The first 50 words of the Body Copy are extremely important. If you keep interest after 50 words, the reader will generally read up to 500 or even 1000 words.

I.   The more facts you tell in the Body Copy , the more product you will sell.

J.   Include testimonials in the Body Copy whenever possible; they increase sales.

K.   Try to use helpful advice in your Body Copy, It increases sales.

ICA and HW 16

Answer the following essays:

1.   Why is the headline the most important part of your ad copy?
2.   Why are free and new the two most powerful words in advertising?

3. Why do longer headlines create more sales than shorter ones?
4. Why should you include your promise and brand in your headline?
5. Why are the first fifty words of your Body Copy the most important part of that section?
6. Why should you include testimonials and advice in your Body Copy?

Additional Internet Resources for this Lesson:

General Resource

http://www.askmrmovies.com

Citizen Kane (1941) – a classic of newspaper advertising

Creating Simple Headlines For Advertising

Suggested Text:
The Art of Plain Talk – Flesch

http://advertising.about.com/od/printadsandflyers/a/writingheadline.htm

Creating Good Copy For Your Advertising

http://suite101.com/article/writing-ads-copy-a152095

Intro to Lesson Seventeen

In this lesson plan outline, Ogilvy takes us through the elusive art of selecting the right photos and creating the right kinds of posters that will drive sales up if executed properly. A picture is worth a thousand words, but only if it is the correct picture. I happen to share Ogilvy's distaste for billboards along the major highways of the US. However, they do produce revenue, so.....

Lesson 17 - How to Illustrate Advertisements and Posters

A.   The subject of your ad is far more important the technique you use to create it.

B.   Ads should work on the curiosity of the viewer. This requires something known as story appeal. Getting the absolute best photographs for your ads and posters are essential just to have a chance at success.

C.   The photographs have to communicate or telegraph your selling promise to the potential client. Avoid being too funny or too artistic in your ad; it will detract from the selling promise.

D.   When you use a photo of a man, you lose a large section of women as potential viewers, if you use a photo of a woman, you lose a substantial part of your male audience. Use a couple whenever selling a neutrally sexual product.

E.   If women are your target, a baby is the best subject. Using sexy women to sell to women does not work as well as using a plain housewife. Color ads are 50% more effective than black and white ads. Crowd ads do not work as well as single subject ads.

F.   Avoid showing buildings and inanimate subjects. Ignore the advice of art directors; they are more concerned with art than selling.

G.   Ads that look like editorial pages make 50%+ more in sales. Make sure your photos have a good caption underneath (and ONLY underneath). Start your copy with a large initial letter. Avoid long paragraphs. The first paragraph should be 12 words or less.

H.   Your copy should be no wider than newspaper articles; that is the highest percentage return on ads for width.

I.   Set your ad in 10 or 11 point type. Smaller type than this sells at a much lower rate. Larger type than this takes up too much room on your ad.
J.   **Using BOLD type is good after three or four paragraphs to break up the monotony of your ad. Also insert illustrations every three or four paragraphs.**
K.   *Use bullets or asterisks * to help your reader into your paragraphs.
L.   Keep to Black on White for ads. Avoid white on black. Avoid colored text.
M.   Your headline should be the same size from start to finish. Avoid ads in CAPS; THEY ARE HARDER TO READ (because we learn to read in lower case).
N.   For coupon ads, put your coupon in the top middle part of your ad and nowhere else.
O.   Project an image of class in your ad. People do not like to be seen consuming products that others regard as second class.
P.   Advertising copy is superior to posters in over 90% of all ads (according to Harvard Business School). Good advertising copy is as rare as good short stories and good novels.
Q.   If you must do a poster, be as outrageous as possible. Use realistic photos and avoid abstracts. You have five seconds for billboard posters. The driver's attention is even less than that in many traffic situations. Use pure strong colors, no more than three colors, and all against a white background. Use the Largest Possible Type with your brand (Coca-Cola) visible (8 words or less).

ICA and HW 17

Answer the following essays:

1.   **Why are the subjects of your ads more important than the technique you use to sell them?**
2.   **Why are curiosity and promise key factors in the development of your ad?**
3.   **Why is photo selection an enormous part of a successful ad campaign?**
4.   **Why should your copy be newspaper width?**
5.   **Why should you avoid using LARGE TYPE in your ads?**
6.   **Why should your copy be very brief for billboards?**

Additional Internet Resources for this Lesson:

General Resource

http://www.askmrmovies.com

Bad Writing (documentary) (2012)

Creating Great Copy For Ads

http://www.streetdirectory.com/travel_guide/5015/marketing/kick_starting_body_copy.html

Creating Great Posters

http://www.ehow.com/video_7369054_design-advertising-poster.html

Intro to Lesson Eighteen

Although we have had fifty years of television ads since the advent of the Ogilvy and Mather advertising agency, there are still some basic, classic rules of thumb to follow on the dos and don'ts of TV advertising. In this lesson plan outline, we examine how to make a good 30 second spot ad.

Lesson 18 – How to Make Good Television Ads

    A.   The purpose of TV advertising is not to ENTERTAIN, but to SELL the product.

B.   Do not use spoken words alone in a spot; make sure you include photo(s). If the customer doesn't see it, they will most likely forget it.

C.   You have exactly 28 seconds for a 30 second spot commercial to communicate all seven of the elements of advertising. Pressure? What pressure? This is what you are getting paid the big bucks for, so don't whine.

D.   Try to make your product NEWS. Use the EDITORIAL approach if possible.

E.   Avoid jingles and clever little sayings like "Just Do It" and "You Deserve A Break Today". They are trite and do not make a promise for the product.

F.   Use Extreme Close-Ups for your TV ads. Most TV screens are not giant-sized. Make sure your product gets a close-up with the name being mentioned as it is photographed.

G.   Sometimes you cannot fit in all seven elements of advertising; fit in as many as you can.

ICA and HW 18

Answer the following essays:

1.   **Why is selling your product more important than entertaining the viewer?**
2.   **Why are pictures or clips essential to your ad?**
3.   **Why is the news or editorial method of advertising one of the most successful approaches for TV ads?**
4.   **Why should you avoid jingles or clever sayings in your ads?**
5.   **Why should you use extreme close-ups of your product in your ads?**
6.   **What should you do if you cannot fit all seven elements of advertising in your ad?**

Additional Internet Resources for this Lesson:

General Resource

http://www.askmrmovies.com

Network (1976) – classic film on TV ads

How to Photograph a TV spot

http://smallbusiness.chron.com/television-advertisement-techniques-18629.html

Editorial Advertising

http://www.theguardian.com/technology/2009/feb/16/netbytes-adverts-aotw

Intro to Lesson Nineteen

Everyone enjoys a good meal. But how do you differentiate your food product from the thousands of others out there in the market? Pay close attention to how Ogilvy can make you want to go out and buy the most mundane foods (like Kraft Miracle Whip). There is a method to his madness.

Lesson 19 – How to Make Good Ad Campaigns For Food Products

    A.   Build your ad around the appetite of the consumer
    B.   Use close-ups of your food and make sure they are appealing
    C.   Don't show people in your food ads; just the food
    D.   Use great photos of your food
    E.   Stick to ONE primary photo
    F.   Have a recipe that includes your food; consumers love recipes
    G.   Don't bury your recipe in the copy; make sure it is isolated
    H.   Print your recipe on white paper; not on the photo or screen
    I.   Get some news into your ad about your food product
    J.   Make your headline specific; not general
    K.   Include your brand name in your headline
    L.   Be serious about food ads; humor or clever copy is not recommended

ICA and HW 19

Answer the following essays:

    1.   **Why should we use the consumer's appetite to sell our product?**
    2.   **Why should people be left out of food commercials?**
    3.   **Why should we primarily use only one photo for our food ad?**
    4.   **Why should we include a recipe when selling our food product?**

5. Why should we eliminate humor from food ads?

Additional Internet Resources for this Lesson:

General Resource

http://www.askmrmovies.com

Hamburger (1986)

How to Create Good Food Ads

http://smashinghub.com/36-most-popular-print-food-advertisements.htm

How to do Food Ads for TV

http://www.creativeblog.com/3d/top-tv-commercials-12121024

Intro to Lesson Twenty (Review Lesson Eight Before Beginning This Lesson)

Ogilvy gives us some sound advice on how to climb the ladder of success in the advertising business. I particularly liked the advice on vacations and, plan to execute them myself. His other advice is just as valuable, so pay attention.

Lesson 20 – How to Climb the Ladder of Success in Advertising

    A.   Be ambitious, but not so ambitious that people around you sense you are ambitious, or they will find ways to sabotage you.

    B.   Be humble when arriving with your fresh MBA from an Ivy-League school; you will be a target from your first day if you are not.

    C.   Learn everything there is to know about your first account including hands-on, in-person visits in addition to internet research.

    D.   Make sure you are an expert at headlines and body copy in addition to your other skills.

    E.   Be a master of presentations

    F.   Keep your client's and potential client's information completely confidential; make believe you are a priest who has heard someone's confession.

    G.   Take a solid two week vacation, without children, but with your wife. Dump the kid(s) at grandma's for the two weeks. Do nothing but eat, sleep and have fun and then come back to your job refreshed.

ICA and HW 20

Answer the following essays:

    1.   Why should we hide our ambition from our fellow office workers?

    2.   Why should we be humble when first entering the new workplace in advertising?

    3.   Why should we make personal visits to our first client (and every client) in addition to internet research?

    4.   Why should we become experts in creating headlines and body text for our ads?

    5.   Why should we maintain confidentiality with our client's information?

6. Why are vacations important in the advertising business?

Additional Internet Resources for this Lesson:

General Resource

http://www.askmrmovies.com

It's a Wonderful Life (1946) – Will give you the proper perspective on ambition

How to Handle Office Politics

http://guides.wsj.com/careers/how-to-overcome-career-obstacles/how-to-handle-office-politics/

Keeping Your Client's Information Confidential

http://www.wisegeek.org/what-is-workplace-confidentiality.htm

Intro to Lesson Twenty-One

Well, hopefully, the previous 20 lessons will give you a nice start on your advertising career in the United States; but what if you are an advertising exec in a place like......China? Here are a few lessons based on an accumulation of five years of research on the subject. China is projected to be the number one trading partner of the US by 2020. You will be selling a lot to them.

Lesson 21 – Selling on TV in China

A.   Selling on TV in China is not like selling on TV anywhere else in the world. It is completely unique to TV advertising, except for the basic elements of ads.

B.   There is primarily only ONE advertising agency for all the CCTV stations in China; that would be the Golden (indeed) Bridge Advertising Agency, which has an unbelievable monopoly on advertising within China.

C.   Despite having a monopoly, Golden Bridge creates numerous spectacular TV spots and ads for its clients; especially in their travel destination advertising. Even products as mundane as mineral water are given first-class treatment by this first-class ad agency.

D.   Spots on Chinese television can vary widely. In the US and most other countries, the average spot is either 15 seconds or 30 seconds. In China, the spot can be as long as two minutes. Most spots are still 15 or 30 seconds, however. There seems to be a bit more room for creativity and varying ad lengths for Chinese television.

E.   Chinese ads often use Western actors and actresses for some reason, even though 99% or more of their consumers are Chinese. I cannot see the economic benefit of using Western words or actors in any Chinese ad. If 95% (5% may understand some very BASIC English in China) of your consumer audience does not understand your ad, you are wasting 95% of your ad budget. Use Chinese characters, Chinese actors and Chinese props to sell American or Western items; your advertising will yield far more in results.

F.   The same spots run over and over again on Chinese television. It is not clear whether this is because there is limited creativity in the advertising sector or whether the companies are pulling in a consistent sales number each month; in which case they would be correct not to fix anything if it is not broken.

G.   The most successful ads are the ones which include items with low unit costs, such as drinking water, iced tea and other simple items. These products have the widest consumer population in China and so targeting them is much easier then, let's say, targeting the right market to sell BMWs.

H.   Buying time in the right time slots is key for many major companies. Chinese audiences love talent programs and they have the highest viewer ratings of all Chinese broadcasts. Consequently, these time slots are the most expensive to advertise in, but you get what you pay for.

I.   Before doing any advertisement you plan to air on CCTV, make sure you comply with all censorship rules BEFORE you air the commercial. The rules are publically listed at the Xinhuanet.com site.

ICA and HW 21

Answer the following essays:

1.   **How do Chinese TV and commercials differ from Western TV and commercials.**
2.   **Why is the Golden Bridge Advertising Agency important in China?**
3.   **Why do many Chinese advertising clients run the same ads over and over again?**
4.   **Why are low unit cost items safer economically to advertise than big ticket items?**
5.   **Why is the right time slot and program very important for the success of your ad?**
6.   **Why should you check with Xinhua web site regulations governing TV advertising before you make your ad?**

Additional Internet Resources for this Lesson:

General Resource

http://www.askmrmovies.com **watch Chinese TV like the Chinese at**

http://www.imdb.com/title/tt1261968/

Best Chinese TV Shows to Advertise On

http://bbs.chinadaily.com.cn/thread-852713-1-1.html

Chinese Television Advertising Regulations

http://news.xinhuanet.com/english/china/2013-01/21/c_132117787.htm

Intro to Lesson Twenty-Two

Selling on the internet in China is like going back ten or fifteen years in time and technology from the US and Western internet market. Most of the sites are, naturally, completely Chinese. Some sites try to combine English and Chinese, but usually wind up with Chinglish (a very bad form of English with horrendous spelling and grammar errors). I would advise a Chinese-only site, unless you are selling Western education, Western travel sites, or Western luxury items. Of course, the best solution would be to have a top Western copy writer and a top Chinese copy writer on the same staff; good luck with that formula. Westerners think they are ad geniuses and Chinese think they are ad geniuses. The fact of the matter is that both of them are wrong the vast majority of the time.

Lesson 22 – Selling on the Internet in China

A.   The internet in China is an interesting challenge for entrepreneurs. It is rather common knowledge that there is an enormous amount of government censorship for various reasons (most of them economic). For example, it behooves the Chinese government to keep out social networks like Facebook off the Chinese internet, so that companies like QQ and Sogou can dominate the social networking market and make money for Chinese companies. The taxes collected on these companies, of course, then go right to the Chinese government. There are many good reasons why the Chinese GNP has dominated the world market for a number of years and this is one of them. China, however, is not the only country that practices this form of protectionism.
B.   Despite the limitations of the internet in China, there are still many web site opportunities for small and medium-sized businesses. The basic principles of web site construction still hold true for China as well as the rest of the world; your site must be well-organized, well-advertised and have a niche, or something different from the many competitors that are online.
C.   The Chinese government is very strict about preventing pornography, scams of any type, the selling of questionable items such as fake brand names or anything that infringes on the intellectual property rights of others (contrary to what you may have heard). Also, famous political names such as Mao Zedong and others cannot be used to sell items on the internet in China.

D.   If you sell your items on the internet, you are responsible to pay the Chinese government a fixed percentage of your sales in taxes. Alibaba and Taobao are two successful internet companies that set the standard for Chinese internet businesses.
E.   It is allowable for your web site to be hosted in other countries outside of China. You are still responsible, however, for Chinese taxes. Chinese web sites should primarily be in Chinese unless your company is selling English language materials or other specific Western goods.
F.   Stores and businesses in China that do not have a functioning web site that creates a reliable revenue stream will be at a disadvantage to those stores and businesses that are able to create successful web sites.

ICA and HW 22

Answer the following essays:

1.   **Why is developing a web site a challenge in China?**
2.   **What are some of the key concerns of the Chinese government about the internet in China?**
3.   **How should you handle the issue of taxes for your successful web site?**
4.   **Why is the language of your web site a major concern?**
5.   **Why do successful business web sites have an advantage over businesses that do not have one?**

Additional Internet Resources for this Lesson:

General Resource

http://www.askmrmovies.com

The Social Network (2010) – Story of Facebook and Mark Zuckerberg fascinating

Chinese Web Sites

http://www.alexa.com/topsites/countries/CN

Chinese Taxes

http://en.wikipedia.org/wiki/Taxation_in_China

Intro to Lesson Twenty-Three

One of my favorite topics in the classroom is the examination of small businesses in China; primarily those who sell in flea markets and in the streets. Believe it or not, these millions of businesses have a much higher success rate than the ones who apply for loans from the Bank of China. Why? Because they are much smaller and include a much lower risk. There are still a significant amount of failures (measured on a three year scale), but the success rate is almost 30% (or more than three times that of bigger businesses). Most of these street vendors do not pay for space or rent. Many have very few expenses outside of their inventory. One of the major drawbacks, however, of these street businesses is the lack of differentiation; you can find a hundred other street vendors selling the same exact items. This leads to about 70% of them eventually getting undersold and going out of business. Another major drawback is the lack of technical expertise among millions of these vendors; many of whom do not have a computer or web site.

Lesson 23 – Selling on the Street in China

A.   Selling on the streets of Chinese cities is one of the more profitable endeavors for many Chinese business people. The risk is lower, there is little or no rent to pay, taxes are seldom, if ever paid, and the success rate of these millions of small businesses is approximately three times higher than bankrolled businesses in China which have a failure rate of 92% within three years according to Bank of China's loan departments.

B.   You need to live in the city you are selling your street goods and be at your table for about twelve hours a day. This can be a demanding, and sometimes unrewarding experience when sales are slow.

C.   Selling on the streets of China is very safe and there is very little theft due to the social mores of the vast majority of Chinese. Bargaining, however, is another ball game altogether. Almost every customer will bargain for almost every item. That is why the original price is never the price the street vendor expects to receive. You can easily expect anywhere from 10-20% every item and up to 50% off if you spend a lot of money.

D.   Chinese street vendors are at the mercy of bad weather, poor location, and competition from 100 other vendors selling the same things they have. This provides the consumer with a lot of ammunition for bargaining. Despite these drawbacks, many street vendors still make a good profit by the end of the day.

E.   If a street vendor is wise enough to have a niche or a bit of differentiation, they will prosper much more than standard street vendors.

F.   Street vendors who are tech savvy AND have a niche will be almost guaranteed to make quite a lot of money. A local web site that is successful in creating a reliable revenue stream in addition to a live location with differentiated goods is a lethal combination in the flea market.

ICA and HW 23

Answer the following essays:

1.   **How do street vendors in China compare with other small and medium-sized businesses in China?**
2.   **Why must you live where you do business as a street vendor in China?**
3.   **How does bargaining enter into the pricing of goods that a street vendor in China has.**
4.   **Why is differentiation a key factor to the success of a Chinese street vendor?**
5.   **How does technical expertise add to the advantage of Chinese street vendor?**

Additional Internet Resources for this Lesson:

General Resource

http://www.askmrmovies.com

Street Life (2006) – a candid look at migrant workers trying to make money as street vendors

Chinese Street Vendors

http://triciawang.com/bytes-of-china/2011/12/19/street-vendor-life-in-china.html

Top Chinese Flea Markets

http://www.tour-beijing.com/blog/beijing-travel/top-10-beijing-markets/

Intro to Lesson Twenty-Four

And of course, there are the regular Chinese shops and stores. These have a success rate a bit higher than bigger businesses, but lower than street vendors because they have to pay rent and usually are not differentiated from dozens of other stores selling exactly the same items in other parts of the city (sometimes on the same block!). Read on before you make a decision to open a store after you graduate from college.

Lesson 24 – Selling in Stores in China

A.   There are three primary groups of stores in China; stores on main streets, stores on side streets, and stores in malls. Stores in malls are almost always expensive, but they are a bit differentiated from most of the other stores in the streets. Stores on the main streets are almost always more expensive than the stores on the side streets and usually have goods that not that well differentiated. Stores on the side streets will almost always be less expensive for the consumer, but will also suffer from a lack of differentiation in most cases.

B.   Mall stores will most often have very high rents to pay and must make X amount in volume sales just to break even. The failure rate of these stores is over 90% according to the Bank of China. Failure usually occurs due to a lack of good advertising, a failure to differentiate, and having a lack of technical expertise to create a successful web site.

C.   Stores located on main streets have a bit higher success rate than the mall stores, but still suffer from the same deficiencies that mall stores have. Their failure rate is over 80%.

D.   Stores located in side streets seem to be a bit more successful than those located on main streets or in the malls because Chinese have learned over the years (as well as foreigners) to shop on side streets to get better bargains and to save money (a Chinese national pastime). The failure rate here is still over 70% due to the same reasons the mall and main street stores fail.

E.   Unlike the flea markets and street vendors, mall stores and main street stores seldom bargain with their goods. You might get an occasional discount, but they will generally stick to their prices because they have overhead factored into the inventory prices.

F.   Side street stores are much more likely to offer customers a discount and are ready to bargain for practically everything they have except for food items.

ICA and HW 24

Answer the following essays:

1. What the three main types of stores in China and how do they differ?
2. What the advantages and disadvantages of a mall store in China?
3. What the advantages and disadvantages of stores located on main streets in China?
4. What the advantages and disadvantages of stores located on side streets in China?
5. How do all three of these types of stores differ from flea markets and street vendors?

Additional Internet Resources for this Lesson:

General Resource

http://www.askmrmovies.com

A Simple Noodle Story (2009) – Good insight on how a native Chinese business is run

Chinese Mall Stores

http://www.chinatouristmaps.com/top-10s/shopping-malls.html

Chinese Stores on Streets (Restaurants)

http://www.simsimhamara.info/chinese-restaurant-business-plans-why-you-need-one/

Epilogue

I hope you have enjoyed your trip through the advertising world. Don't let the fearful numbers of failure stop you from trying your hand at advertising. Better to have tried and failed than to never have tried at all. The same holds true for trying your own business. Follow your bliss as one great man once said. Life is a long road; get off onto one of the sidestreets and do a little shopping for fun.